James Lee

D1147466

ESSENTIALS
GCSE Study Skills

Contents

4 Introduction

Self Management

6 Goal-Setting

12 Time Management

18 Stress Management

24 Group Study

Developing a File of Revision Notes

30 Reading

36 Note-Taking

42 Summary Sheets

48 Mnemonics

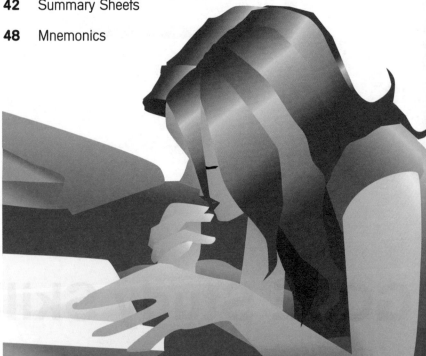

Revising Subjects

54 English

58 Maths

62 Science

66 Modern Languages

70 Geography

74 History

The Exams

78 Coursework Projects

84 Exam Technique

90 Revision Strategy

Contents

Introduction

The day that you collect or download your GCSE results will inevitably be one of the most significant moments in your life. Achieving a good set of GCSE grades will provide you not only with a passport to further education, but also with a long-lasting sense of accomplishment and self-confidence. Conversely, failing to fulfil your academic potential can lead to a deep and lasting sense of regret and to you missing out on the opportunities enjoyed by other young people.

This book teaches you the **study skills** that you need to achieve GCSE success. Some of these skills will help you to be better organised and to make the best use of resources (e.g. goal-setting, time management, stress management and group study). Other skills will help you to study topics related to each of the subjects that you're taking (e.g. reading, note-taking and mnemonics) – or to master the process of taking and passing exams (e.g. exam technique).

When trying out techniques in this book, remember that we all have unique learning styles – so keep an open mind and use the advice offered here to develop your own unique approach to GCSE revision.

Wishing you every success!

The Structure of this Book

This book is divided up into four distinct sections:

Section 1: Self Management
The first section teaches you how to...

- overcome limiting beliefs, set goals and monitor progress (**goal-setting**)
- change your daily routine, create revision timetables and become more assertive (**time management**)
- reduce exam stress (**stress management**)
- make best use of social learning environments, such as lessons and out-of-school revision get-togethers (**group study**).

Section 2: Developing a File of Revision Notes
The second section teaches you how to use **mnemonics** and outlines various **reading** and **note-taking** techniques (e.g. lists, shapes and maps), which you can use to develop a file of revision notes that summarise each of the topics in the subjects you're taking.

Section 3: Revising Subjects
The third section teaches you how to apply the techniques outlined in Section 2 when revising six particular subject areas: **English, Maths, Science, Modern Foreign Languages, Geography** and **History**.

Section 4: The Exams
The fourth and final section teaches you how to plan, conduct and write-up research projects when completing **coursework**, and outlines a variety of ways in which you can improve your **exam technique**. It concludes with advice on how to write a short summary of your **revision strategy**.

 Now, skim through the various sections of this book before taking a closer look at each unit.

Goal-Setting

There are things you can do to improve your goal-setting skills. This unit focuses on examining the core principles of effective goal-setting.

The Bigger Picture

As illustrated below, one way of thinking about GCSE success is as the first in a number of stepping-stones leading to the realisation of your long-term goals.

- Imagine, for example, that you aim to inspire people by directing blockbuster movies. Access to a local FE college could provide you with the qualifications needed to gain a place at film-school which could, in turn, provide you with the knowledge and skills needed to work in the film industry.
- Or imagine that you want to promote fair-trade by working for an organisation that runs projects in developing countries. GCSE success could enable you to secure a work experience placement that provides you with the expertise and contacts required to get a job working for an international charity when you leave university.

The Reflective Cycle

As illustrated below, effective goal-setting can be split into four stages that are jointly known as **the reflective cycle**:

Stage 1: Vision
Generating a positive vision of the accomplishment of your goals and reinforcing this regularly (e.g. through completing visualisation exercises)

Stage 4: Evaluation
Monitoring your progress to help refine your vision and plan (e.g. completing entries in a revision diary)

Stage 2: Plan
Developing a strategy (e.g. creating a revision timetable and listing equipment that you will need when revising)

Stage 3: Action
Taking positive action (e.g. getting-up half an hour earlier every day to review your revision notes)

The rest of this unit looks at each of these stages in more detail.

Stage 1: Generating a Vision

If someone asks you not to think of a red apple then what's the first thing you think of? A red apple! The mind finds it difficult to 'negate' negative thoughts so it's best to focus on the positive.

Positive Visualisation Exercises

Here's an example of how you might use visualisation exercises on a daily basis during the run-up to your exams:

1. Sit-up on your bed or sit on a chair and close your eyes.
2. Relax your muscles, take a few slow and deep breaths and, with each out-breath, count down from 10 to 1.
3. Imagine that it's the day your GCSE results are released and you open the letter (or email) confirming that you've been awarded the very best GCSE grades you believe you can achieve.
4. Before opening your eyes, close this exercise by saying to yourself three times, 'I am capable of achieving these grades in my GCSEs'.

You could also run through similar exercises by imagining yourself feeling relaxed and confident in the exam room – or leaving your last exam feeling a great sense of relief and joy.

Exercises of this sort are most effective when completed daily, when you hold, for at least one minute, the positive vision of yourself achieving your ideal grades, when your vision is as clear and intense as possible and when you feel certain that it'll actually happen on the day your results are released.

Stage 2: Making a Plan

Trying to prepare for your GCSEs without making a plan is like attempting to walk from one end of the country to the other without a map! Instead, develop a revision strategy. A good place to start is by thinking about available resources.

Space – The ideal space for revision has plenty of natural sunlight and is quiet, spacious and cool, but not cold. Which rooms in your house have these qualities? Are there ways that you could reorganise your room? If home isn't good for revision then you may need to work somewhere else, such as a local library.

Time – Think about how to make best use of time between now and your exams. Key aspects of effective time management include: clarifying priorities; creating a timetable; changing your daily routine; and being assertive. The next unit of this book looks at all of these in more detail.

Money – There are essential pieces of revision equipment, such as stationery (e.g. pens, notebooks, files) and publications (e.g. revision guides and exam papers). It's therefore worth setting aside money (or asking your parents for some money) to top-up your 'revision kit'.

People – Ask teachers and smart students for help, revise outside of school with friends, and discuss with family members any problems that you're experiencing. You could also ask teachers about the additional support your school offers to exam-year students.

Stage 3: Taking Action

Preparing for GCSEs is more like completing a long distance run than a short sprint. Having got started, you'll soon realise that it's one thing to muster-up the energy required to complete a day or two of intensive revision, but quite another to sustain the patience, stamina and self-discipline required to carefully work through each of your subjects over several months.

Despite all the best intentions, at times, your perseverance will inevitably be severely tested. The key is to keep a broader perspective on how your revision is progressing, to focus on solutions rather than problems, to stay relaxed and to continue revising!

Transforming Limiting Beliefs

Limiting beliefs are false assumptions about yourself and the world. Changing your beliefs can transform your capacity to prepare for your GCSEs.

- **Limiting Belief 1:** 'I'm rubbish at exams'.
  Positive Response: 'Exam success isn't just about being clever, but about working hard and improving my study skills. By following advice in this book and applying myself I can achieve higher grades'.
- **Limiting Belief 2:** 'I don't have enough time to revise'.
  Positive Response: 'I can make simple changes to my daily routine. If I get up earlier on weekdays and pack-in my Saturday job for a couple of months, this will give me more time to revise'.

>> Now identify 5–10 of your limiting beliefs about revision and exams, and write down some positive responses.

Stage 4: Evaluating Progress

The last of the four stages of effective goal-setting involves regularly (e.g. at the end of each day or week) setting aside time to review recent experiences, to evaluate how revision is progressing and to use this process to refine your vision, amend your strategy and take fresh action, etc.

One way to simplify this process is by keeping a revision diary. Each entry could be structured around a collection of headings (e.g. 'How I'm Feeling') or might take the form of a flow of whatever thoughts come into your mind at any particular time.

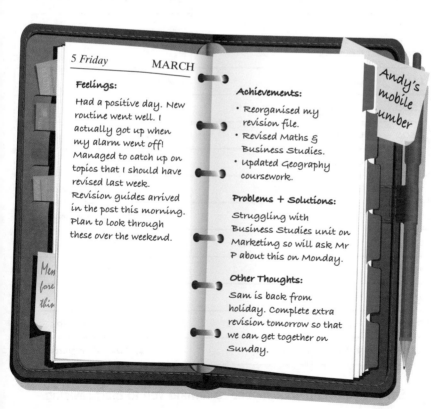

5 Friday   MARCH

Feelings:

Had a positive day. New routine went well. I actually got up when my alarm went off! Managed to catch up on topics that I should have revised last week. Revision guides arrived in the post this morning. Plan to look through these over the weekend.

Achievements:

- Reorganised my revision file.
- Revised Maths & Business Studies.
- Updated Geography coursework.

Problems + Solutions:

Struggling with Business Studies unit on Marketing so will ask Mr P about this on Monday.

Other Thoughts:

Sam is back from holiday. Complete extra revision tomorrow so that we can get together on Sunday.

Andy's mobile number

Time Management

Students typically need 30–90 minutes to properly revise each of the 200–300 topics in the subjects they're taking. This means setting aside at least 200 hours and revising for an average of 1–2 hours per day from 3–6 months before your exams start!

Changing Your Daily Routine

A good way to find time for revision is by changing your routine:
1. Create a table like the one below and note down your typical activities.
2. Make changes that enable you to revise for 1–2 hours per day.

Time	Weekdays	Weekends
0800	Travel to school	Get ready / Have breakfast
0900	Lessons	Revision
1000	Lessons	Revision
1100	Lessons	Travel into town
1200	Lessons	Go to the gym
1300	Lunch	Go to the gym
1400	Lessons	Lunch
1500	Football practice	Shopping / Socialising
1600	Football practice	Shopping / Socialising
1700	Walk home with Sam	Shopping / Socialising
1800	Dinner	Travel from town
1900	Homework	Dinner
2000	Revision	Out with Sam / friends
2100	Relax / My time	Out with Sam / friends

 Set the alarm on your mobile to remind you to start revising.

Estimating Your Revision Time

Before doing anything else, check that your new daily routines are ambitious, but realistic. After making some final adjustments, you can estimate the total amount of time available for revision:

1 Multiply the time that you intend to revise on average each day by the total number of days between now and your first exam.

15 weeks until my first exam
15 x 5 = 75 weekdays x 2 hours = 150 hours on weekdays
15 Saturdays x 3 hours = 45 hours on Saturdays
15 Sundays x 3 hours = 45 hours on Sundays

2 Add these three totals together.

150 hours + 45 hours + 45 hours = 240 hours

3 Subtract the number of days when you know that it will be difficult for you to revise (e.g. if you're going to a wedding).

Unavailable on 5 weekdays x 2 hours = 10 hours
Unavailable on 5 Saturdays or Sundays x 3 hours = 15 hours
Unavailable for a total of 10 hours + 15 hours = 25 hours
Total time available: 240 hours – 25 hours = 215 hours

4 Assume you've underestimated the number of days when it will be difficult for you to revise by reducing this figure by 10–20 hours.

Total revision time: 215 hours – 15 hours = **200 hours**

Distributing Your Time Across Subjects

To make sure that you don't spend too much time revising certain subjects (e.g. the ones that you find easiest), it's important that you share out total revision time across all the subjects you're studying. Create a table like this one:

Subject	Topics	Revision Time	
		In Total	Per Topic
English	15	20 hours	80 mins
Maths	40	20 hours	30 mins
Chemistry	30	20 hours	40 mins
Physics	20	20 hours	1 hour
Biology	20	20 hours	1 hour
ICT	20	20 hours	1 hour
French	20	20 hours	1 hour
Design	30	20 hours	40 mins
Geography	20	20 hours	1 hour
History	20	20 hours	1 hour

As there are more topics in some subjects than others, it's also helpful, at this stage, to make a note of the number of topics you need to revise for each subject. You can then use these figures to work out roughly how much time you need to spend revising each topic within each subject.

Distributing Your Time Across Topics

Having calculated how long you need to spend revising 'typical' topics, you can decide whether particular topics deserve special attention.

For example, imagine that you aim to spend 20 hours revising English. There are 15 topics in your English syllabus so a typical English topic should take 80 minutes to revise. But, you missed the lesson on 'advertising' so you decide to spend more time revising this topic, and you focused on 'travel writing' and 'magazines' in your coursework so you set aside less time to revise these topics (see table below).

Topic	In Total
1. Writing to imagine and explore	80 mins
2. Writing to inform and describe	80 mins
3. Writing to explain and advise	80 mins
4. Writing to argue and persuade	80 mins
5. Writing to analyse and review	80 mins
6. Newspapers	80 mins
7. Advertising	120 mins
8. Film and television	80 mins
9. Magazines	50 mins
10. Biographies	80 mins
11. Travel writing	50 mins
12. Shakespeare	80 mins
13. Drama texts	80 mins
14. Novels and short stories	80 mins
15. Poetry	80 mins
TOTAL	20 hours

Creating Revision Timetables

When creating revision timetables, rather than trying to revise *all* your subjects *every* week, focus on revising half of the subjects you're taking one week and the other half the following week, etc.

	English	Maths	Biology	French	Geography	TOTAL
Mon.		Fractions (1 hour)			Settlement (1 hour)	2 hours
Tues.			Enzymes (1 hour)	Transport (1 hour)		2 hours
Wed.	Travel writing (1 hour)				Trade / Aid (1 hour)	2 hours
Thurs.		Vectors (1 hour)		Sport (1 hour)		2 hours
Fri.	Attending Open Day at Stonebridge FE College					0 hours
Sat.	Poetry (1 hour)	Triangles (1 hour)			Volcanoes (1 hour)	3 hours
Sun.			Disease (2 hours)	Holidays (1 hour)		3 hours
TOTAL	2 hours	3 hours	3 hours	3 hours	3 hours	14 hours

A revision timetable tells you what you need to revise each day and puts you in control of your revision. Don't worry if at any point you get behind. By working towards revising all topics by your first exam, you can catch up between exams.

Make a revision timetable using Microsoft Word™, or use the ready-made calendars in Microsoft Publisher™.

Be Assertive

Once you've created and committed to your new daily routines and revision timetable, you'll soon realise that, in order to stick to them, you'll need to…

- resist temptations to do things that you find easier or more enjoyable (e.g. having a lie-in, watching TV, chatting on the phone)
- overcome pressures from other people (e.g. just before you start revising, you receive a text inviting you to meet up with a friend)
- be assertive (e.g. get better at saying things like, 'I'm revising this morning. How about meeting up this afternoon instead?').

Competing Priorities

Rank the activities listed below from 1–8 according to how important they are to you between now and your last exam (1 = most important; 8 = least important).

- doing paid work to earn some extra cash
- keeping fit and playing sports
- spending time with family
- doing voluntary work for local charities
- getting at least 8 hours' sleep every night
- going shopping
- socialising with friends.
- studying and revising for my exams

This exercise highlights that GCSE success is only one of a number of competing priorities in your life. The key is to assert your need to revise without neglecting other things that are important to you.

Stress Management

Stress-Busting Techniques

When people suffer from stress their concentration is poor and they find it difficult to memorise and recall information. Long periods of stress will have a negative impact on the effectiveness of your revision and on your performance in the exam room. This unit outlines five stress-busting techniques:

Avoid major life changes

Complete revision diary entries

Stress-Busting Techniques

Create a positive revision environment

Develop a social support network

Improve your health and fitness

1. Major Life Changes

Can you remember your first day at secondary school? How did you feel when you arrived? Starting a new school is an example of a major life change. Such changes can trigger stress so, if possible, they're best avoided during the run-up to exams.

Examples of Major Life Changes

- Moving house
- Being dumped by your boyfriend or girlfriend
- Starting a new relationship
- Taking up a work experience placement
- Starting a new Saturday job
- Setting-up a new club or society
- Playing for a new sports team
- Agreeing to play a lead role in the school musical
- Borrowing money to buy something expensive
- Going on holiday to somewhere you've never been before

Some of these life changes are likely to be largely beyond your control (e.g. your parents deciding to sell your house). And remember that even 'positive' changes, such as a new relationship or a new job, can trigger stress.

The key is not to try to avoid every source of stress, but to be sensible about how many life changes you make whilst preparing for your GCSEs.

2. Revision Environments

Clearing and re-organising a room that you use as your primary out-of-school revision space (e.g. your bedroom) will help to put you in control of your revision, and will boost your self-confidence. When rearranging your room, remember that positive learning environments have four principal qualities:

1 **Space** – Trying to revise in a small, cluttered room can make you feel tense and claustrophobic. Good revision environments have ample floor and desk space, and are clear of rubbish, junk and bric-a-brac. Maybe now is the perfect time to take some stuff to a charity shop!

2 **Light** – It's best to revise in a room that has plenty of natural sunlight (e.g. that has a big window). If this isn't possible then buy brighter bulbs for the lights in your room or get a nice new desk lamp.

3 **Noise** – The sounds of radios, traffic and people talking can make it difficult to read, think and concentrate. If you have a TV in your room turn it off when you're revising and keep the volume of music to a minimum.

4 **Temperature** – Very warm rooms can make you feel agitated or sleepy so, if necessary, keep the temperature down in your room by opening the window or buying a fan. It's better to wear warm clothes in a cool room than to attempt to revise in a furnace!

3. Health and Fitness

Because of the strong links between mind and body, one of the best ways to combat exam stress is by ensuring that you keep yourself physically fit and healthy.

Eat a Balanced Diet – Note down everything you've eaten and drunk over the last two days. Does it include a balance of the main food groups? Or do you mainly eat junk food and sugary snacks? Research shows that people concentrate better when they drink plenty of water. How about meals? Do you eat three meals a day or have you got into the habit of snacking?

Take Regular Exercise – Note down all the different forms of exercise (e.g. walking, going for a jog, football, swimming, etc.) you've done over the last seven days and how long each session lasted. Do you do at least 30 minutes' exercise a day? Are there other simple opportunities for you to get more exercise (e.g. taking the dog for walks or joining the local sports centre)?

Get Plenty of Rest / Sleep – Finally, make a note of the times that you went to bed and got-up over the last five days. Do you go to bed and get up at the same time each day or are your sleep patterns irregular? What's the minimum length of sleep that you need in order to feel refreshed in the morning? Do you find time each day to relax? Why not try getting up an hour earlier for the next few days?

4. Social Support Networks

Imagine that your school sends you to revise on a desert island. There's plenty of clean water, food and shelter, and you arrive with all the equipment that you need, but there are no people! Think about how you'll lose out if you isolate yourself from other people during the run-up to your exams.

Stay Connected

Some of the best ways to reduce exam stress involve other people, so be sure to stay connected to your family, friends and teachers.

- Text, phone and email your friends.
- Enjoy a meal with your family.
- Go for walks with your friends.
- Ask classmates if you can borrow their notes or revision guides.
- Ask family members what they did to reduce stress when revising.
- Get together with friends to revise.
- Invite yourself round to your grandparents' house for a cup of tea.
- Ask your boyfriend / girlfriend to give you a hug.
- Reward yourself by going to the cinema with your best friend.
- Ask your teacher questions during, and at the end of, lessons.
- Book an appointment to see your tutor or school counsellor if revision gets you down.

5. Revision Diary Entries

Completing regular entries in a revision diary provides you with the chance to review your progress and reflect on solutions to any difficulties you're facing (see page 11). It also provides opportunities for you to complete and write up exercises that'll help you to pacify negative emotions and stay positive.

1 Recall a recent incident that provoked strong emotions

> Last night Dad told me that I couldn't go out because, I'm 'not taking my revision seriously'. We started shouting and I locked myself in my room. He left early today so I haven't spoken to him since then.

2 Explain the causes of these emotions

> This incident made me really angry because I have actually been revising for 2 hours every night this week, but Dad doesn't realise because I always revise when he's at work.

3 Describe how you felt at this time

> I felt really tense and as if I was about to explode!

4 Identify the consequences of this incident

> I didn't meet-up with friends and there were so many thoughts running through my head that I couldn't work. I got to sleep late so now I'm feeling really tired.

5 State what you can do to resolve this situation

> I need to talk with Dad tonight. I'll tell him how much work I've been doing and explain that I need regular breaks. We need to find a better way to communicate.

Group Study

Effective revision is not only about studying alone, but also about making the most of social learning environments. such as classrooms. This unit offers advice on how best to integrate opportunities for group study into your revision programme.

Self Study and Group Study

Some aspects of revision (e.g. studying textbooks) are best completed alone in a quiet space where there are few distractions. This is known as **self study**.

Other aspects of revision (e.g. enhancing your existing knowledge of topics) are best-suited to social environments where you can learn more interactively (e.g. by asking and answering questions). This is known as **group study**.

The secret is to find ways to actively link these two distinct, but equally important, aspects of your revision.

Building on Classwork

Imagine that you had a geography lesson on 'tourism' this morning, in which you examined the **consequences** for less developed countries of the fact that the popularity of tourist holidays has significantly increased over recent decades. You might produce notes like these:

1 Positive Consequences

a) Increased foreign investment and new employment opportunities

b) Greater cross-cultural understanding

2 Negative Consequences

a) Damage to the physical environment (e.g. soil erosion and pollution)

b) Human rights abuses (e.g. forced relocation of local residents)

To reinforce and enhance your knowledge and understanding of this topic, during the self study revision session that you complete this evening, you could…

- make-up a mnemonic to help remember some of the positive and negative consequences of the recent growth of tourism
- focus on a particular area that you found difficult to understand or that you feel deserves closer attention
- create a single-page 'summary sheet' that summarises all of the key points in the class notes that you took during this lesson
- search through other sources of information (e.g. websites) to find articles that offer good examples of the consequences of the growth of tourism
- use practice exam papers and past exam papers to answer exam questions about the consequences of the growth of tourism.

Reinforcing Self Study

Imagine that you know your teacher plans to teach 'disease' in tomorrow's biology class so you make time tonight to take notes that sum-up the main points covered in this section of the biology syllabus:

1 Causes of Disease

a) The body is an ideal place for harmful microorganisms (e.g. bacteria, fungi, viruses) to replicate.
b) The damage to cells, and release of toxins, by these microorganisms causes symptoms of disease (e.g. nausea, rashes, pain).

2 The Body's Defences Against Disease

a) Physical barriers (e.g. the skin) and chemical barriers (e.g. the chemicals in sweat and the chemicals in the stomach).
b) White blood cells: i) Phagocytes (engulf and digest microorganisms); ii) Lymphocytes (release antibodies that help to destroy microorganisms).

During the biology lesson you then improve your knowledge and understanding of this topic by…

- asking your teacher probing questions that expand on information in your self-study notes (e.g. 'If white blood cells help to fight disease then why are some diseases treated with drugs that reduce the number of white cells in the blood?')
- recording on rough paper any new information mentioned by your teacher during the lesson (e.g. particular examples of bacteria, fungi and viruses)
- asking your teacher at the end of class to identify important points that you've failed to include in your self-study notes (e.g. reasons why the body is an ideal place for microorganisms to replicate).

The Interactive Classroom

In an ideal classroom, everyone is focused on what they're supposed to be learning and all class members respect and trust each other. The **high rapport relations** between class members create an open and interactive learning environment where students feel free to ask, and respond to, questions, and to actively participate in class discussions. Learning in classrooms like this is very effective and fast!

The 'Wheel of Needs'

All these qualities are present in a high rapport relationship. If any are missing, then the wheel doesn't turn and the relationship doesn't work!

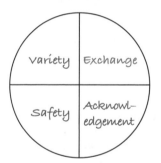

Building Rapport

To ensure that you help create **interactive** lessons, apply the four qualities of the high rapport relationship outlined in the diagram above:

- Create opportunities for two-way **exchange** (e.g. answer questions during lessons and ask questions at the end of lessons).
- Make other students feel **acknowledged** (e.g. value classmates' contributions to discussions by not talking whilst they're speaking).
- Ensure everyone feels **safe** (i.e. don't behave in a threatening manner).
- Remember that **variety** enriches relations (e.g. help maintain a light, open and happy class environment through appropriate use of humour).

Revision Get-Togethers

Organising out-of-school revision get-togethers will help you to build on the work that you complete in lessons, and to expand on progress that you make during self-study sessions at home. One way to plan get-togethers is by answering a few key questions.

1 Who should I invite?

Not Sam, because we'd just talk about things that have nothing to do with revision. Charlie, Ben and Vicky are taking their revision seriously and would be up for it.

2 When should we meet?

On Saturday mornings for a couple of hours.

3 Where should we meet?

At a local café or at Vicky's house, because there's plenty of space for us to meet there.

4 What could we do in advance?

The night before we could each spend an hour revising a different topic.

5 How should the meeting be structured?

We could take it in turns to talk through the topic we revised the night before and then answer questions that other people ask about this topic.

6 Any other thoughts?

We all have Science together with Mr Dobson tomorrow so at the end of the lesson I can ask everyone what they think of this whole idea.

Teaching Topics to Friends

One of the most effective ways to learn information is by teaching and explaining it to others. Here are a few principles to follow when deciding how best to present a topic to friends during revision get-togethers:

1 Create a summary

Arrive at the meeting with a single piece of paper that sums up everything you want to say. You can refer to this sheet whilst teaching and give copies to the other people attending.

2 Divide up the topic into sections

Study your class notes, textbooks and revision guides to identify main sections of the topic that you've agreed to teach.

3 Give examples of exam questions

Have a look through practice and past exam papers so that, towards the end of your presentation, you can give examples of exam questions related to your topic that have cropped up in previous years.

4 Provide opportunities for questions and answers

Encourage questions. Make a note of questions that you found difficult to answer and ask your friends to correct you if they think you've made a mistake or haven't explained something well. Remember, the purpose of these sessions isn't to pretend you're an expert, but to improve your knowledge and understanding of topics that you're learning.

Set-up new email contact groups and use social-networking sites to exchange revision notes and exam questions with friends.

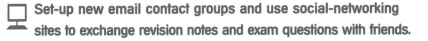

Reading

You'll need to read through all of your class notes, textbooks and revision guides during the run-up to your exams. This section highlights some of the key principles of effective reading.

Using a Reading Guide

Have a go at this exercise: ask someone to draw an imaginary circle in the air simply by rolling their eyes around in a circular fashion. Watch the movements of their eyes as they complete this task.

Now, ask them to allow their eyes to follow the end of your pen as you use it to draw an imaginary circle in the air. Again, watch the movement of their eyes.

Finally, swap around so that they can watch your eye movements.

You should have found that their eyes moved more smoothly when they followed your pen. This is because, without some sort of 'guide', your eyes tend to dart around. Use a pen to guide your eyes across the page as you read. Don't use a bookmark though, as this will obstruct your peripheral vision.

Approaches to Reading

When using a reading guide, there are a variety of techniques that you can use:

1 Reading from left to right

This is the most typical reading approach and is good for tasks that require you not only to identify the broad structure of a text, but also to improve your knowledge and understanding of details (e.g. when carefully studying textbooks and revision guides).

2 Reading from top to bottom

Because we find it difficult to hold more than a few centimetres of text within our focus of vision, this approach is normally only suited to reading texts that have been split into columns (e.g. some newspapers, magazines and website pages).

3 Reading diagonally

You could experiment with using this approach when scanning a text to find specific pieces of information (e.g. when reading lots of different information sources before writing up a coursework report).

Skim-Reading

Some aspects of your revision (e.g. completing an initial overview of a topic before studying it in detail) require you to read lots of information quickly. This is known as skim-reading. Here are some guidelines for skim-reading texts:

Set time constraints – Limit the time you spend skim-reading. If you aim to revise a topic for an hour, set aside five minutes to skim-read it first.

Increase the pace at which you read – Read the following sentence very slowly (i.e. sounding-out each word): 'When promoting new products companies rely on various forms of advertising such as TV adverts and billboards'. Now read the same sentence at your normal reading pace. Comprehension levels go down when people read too slowly, so read at pace when skim-reading.

Skip sections that are difficult to understand – Skip parts of the text that are initially difficult to understand and make a note to come back to these later on.

Jot down notes on rough paper – As you read through the text, underline sub-headings and key words and jot down information you feel is important.

Summarise in your own words – Reinforce your knowledge and understanding of the text by writing a summary of it in your own words.

If you were asked to complete a jigsaw, how would you get started?

- Would you randomly pick up any piece and then sort through the box trying to find pieces that connect to this?

- Or would you extract the side pieces and then join these together to develop a larger framework from which to work?

One way to study a topic is by treating it like a jigsaw. First, read through it at pace and jot down rough notes. Then, fill-in the gaps in your knowledge and understanding by reading it more carefully.

Here's an example of what your rough notes might look like after skim-reading an ICT topic:

Risks	Remedies
1. ☹ STRESS/ANXIETY – new ICT at work	Train employees 2 use new ICT
2. Muscle strain – REPETITIVE STRAIN INJURY	Regular breaks ☺ + ERGONOMIC equipment
3. EYE STRAIN 👁 + headaches	ANTI-GLARE SCREENS + natural sunlight ☼
4. ✗ Electric shock – exposed wires	Replace Wiring Regularly
5. System failures '?!' – public services	AIR TRAFFIC CONTROL controlled by TWO independent computer systems

Reading for Close Analysis

Having overviewed topics by applying skim-reading techniques, you can use skills of close analysis to focus on the details. This approach to reading requires you to…

- annotate texts using key words and symbols
- group information into categories or themes
- think about how to organise your notes.

1 Annotate texts using key words and symbols

As you read through class notes and books, underline **key words**. But, make sure you don't underline too many words – there are normally only **two** or **three** key words in a paragraph and sometimes none at all. Draw **symbols** in the margins to act as **reminders** of important information in each paragraph.

2 Group information into categories or themes

Group information under headings, for example, having read sections of your English notes and revision guides on 'advertising', you conclude that this topic covers issues and techniques relating to three main themes:

- The key features of adverts
- How to analyse adverts that promote products
- How to analyse adverts that encourage people to donate to charity.

3 Think about how to organise your notes

Think about the best way to organise the notes you're going to take on the topic you're revising. There are lots of different options and the next couple of units of this book examine some of these in more detail.

Knowledge and Understanding

Reading for close analysis requires you to generate a more sophisticated knowledge and understanding of topics by contrasting and linking information **as you read**. One way to practise this is by numbering passages of text.

For example, take a look at the history text below on the peace treaty that was signed at the end of World War I. Sentences numbered…

1 relate to who was to blame for the start of the war

2 link to the compensation that Germany was required to pay

3 relate to the weakening of the German army

4 link to the redistribution of land to other countries.

Issues Agreed in the Peace Treaty

1 The Allies made Germany accept blame for starting the war, 2 demanded that Germany pay massive compensation for damage resulting from the war 3 and insisted that Germany's military was weakened. 4 Germany also lost land to Belgium, Denmark, France and Poland.

German Reactions to the Peace Treaty

1 Germans were resentful because they felt several countries were to blame for the war. 4 Due to the redistribution of land, many Germans were also angered by the fact that they were ruled by foreigners. 3 In addition, Germans felt humiliated by the weakening of their armed forces 2 and attempts to pay reparations by printing money led to inflation and unemployment.

Note-Taking

This unit teaches you the essentials of effective note-taking and illustrates how your notes can be used to develop a 'revision file'.

Note-Taking Essentials

Although there's no single note-taking technique that suits every individual or every learning task, there are general principles that you can apply when taking notes. You can think of these principles as a collection of 'tools'.

Colour

One of the simplest and most powerful secrets of effective note-taking involves using colour to highlight, contrast and group information. Some examples of the effective use of colour when revising include…

- highlighting or underlining information according to its importance (e.g. **red** for very important information, **blue** for important information and **green** for quite important information)

- using colours to distinguish between sections of a topic (e.g. **orange** for notes relating to one section and **pink** for notes relating to another section).

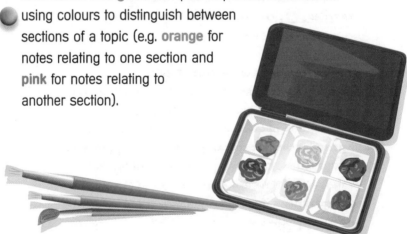

Key Words

You can create memorable notes by using key words. Read the sentences from a business studies topic in the table below. Now cover-up the right-hand column and use the key words in the left-hand column to help you remember what each sentence stated.

Key Words	Sentences
1. PLC 2. Ltd	There are two types of limited company: 1) <u>public limited companies</u> (PLC); and 2) <u>private limited companies</u> (Ltd).
TWO Shareholders	To <u>set-up</u> a public limited company or a private limited company, a minimum of <u>two shareholders</u> is needed.
a) Owners = Shareholders b) Managers = Directors	A limited company is <u>owned</u> by its <u>shareholders</u>, but <u>managed</u> by its <u>directors</u>.
Audited Accounts	The <u>accounts</u> of limited companies have to be audited – <u>checked for accuracy and truthfulness</u> – by external auditors.

Symbols

Your revision notes can also be enhanced by using symbols. In the table above, rather than writing 'two shareholders' you could draw two faces – and rather than writing 'audited accounts' you could draw a piece of paper with a tick on it.

Note-Taking Techniques

Experiment with different ways of summarising a passage of information. For example, the information about the life of Princess Diana in the table below could be summarised in…

- a **list**
- an **eight-part shape**
- a **map**.

1/7/61	Born on 1st July 1961
← Parents 67 →	Parents separated in 1967
Althorp 75	Moved to her family's stately home (Althorp) in 1975
Married 81	Married Prince Charles in 1981
W82	Prince William was born in 1982
H84	Prince Harry was born in 1984
← Charles 92 →	Announced her separation from Prince Charles in 1992
RIP 97	Tragically died in a car crash in Paris in 1997

1. Summary Lists

The key words from the table above could be presented as a list:

Before becoming a Royal:
- 1/7/61
- ← Parents 67 →
- Althorp 75

After becoming a Royal:
- Married 81
- W82
- H84
- ← Charles 92 →
- RIP 97

2. Summary Shapes

Alternatively, you could present these key words in or around an eight-part shape:

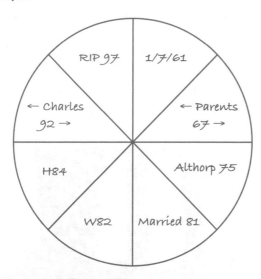

3. Summary Maps

Or, you could present these key words on top of the branches of a two-part map:

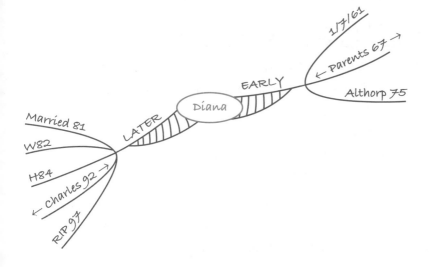

Revision Notes

One of the best ways to generate a good knowledge and understanding of each of the subjects that you're taking is by using a range of note-taking techniques to develop a revision file.

Your revision file should eventually include a single page that summarises each topic you need to revise (e.g. if there are 30 topics in your History syllabus then there should be 30 pieces of paper in the History section of your revision file, etc).

Your Revision File

Having purchased a few pieces of equipment (e.g. a file or portfolio, some file dividers, a set of fine-point coloured pens, plain A4 and A3 paper), all you need to do is...

- choose any topic
- create a single page summary of this topic
- put this summary in your file.

By working through a few topics each day, you'll gradually develop a valuable set of revision notes that you can use regularly to review and test your knowledge and understanding.

Additional Sections

The development of your revision file should be a central focus of your revision. The fact that you'll refer to this file most days also makes it the perfect place to keep a copy of your revision strategy and to store exam papers.

Part 1: Revision Strategy

A copy of your revision strategy can go at the front of your file and should include a brief outline of...

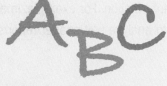

- your goals (e.g. grades that you aim to get in your exams)
- how you intend to make best use of your time (e.g. a revision timetable)
- what you'll do to reduce exam stress (e.g. your exercise regime)
- how you intend to revise with friends out of school (e.g. at your house on Saturday mornings).

Part 2: Summary Sheets

The main body of your revision file should include a one-page summary of each of the topics that you're required to revise for your GCSE exams.

Part 3: Exam Papers

The final section of your file could hold a collection of exam papers. Looking through these will remind you of the format of each paper and will familiarise you with the types of questions examiners are likely to ask.

 Your revision file is a priceless resource, so be sure to look after it!

Summary Sheets

This unit offers detailed advice on how to use three particular note-taking techniques when building-up a collection of summary sheets for your revision file.

Summary Lists

The most traditional way of creating summary sheets involves listing information. For example, imagine that during an English lesson on how to analyse newspaper reports your teacher gave you the handout below:

Analysing newspaper reports

EFFECT
BIAS
Opinions
Theories
Facts

There are different ways of approaching the analysis of newspaper reports. You could compare two reports in terms of their overall <u>effect</u> on the reader or you could look for evidence of <u>bias</u> (e.g. strong <u>opinions</u> and <u>theories</u> but not many <u>facts</u>).

PARTS
Headings
Content
Photos, etc.
Captions

When examining newspaper reports, it is helpful to begin by focusing on principal <u>parts</u> of each article such as its <u>headings</u> and sub-headings, <u>content</u> (i.e. the main body of text) and any <u>photographs</u> or illustrations as well as the <u>captions</u> next to these.

TONE
TECHNIQUES
Simile
Metaphor

Examine the overall <u>tone</u> of language used in newspaper reports (e.g. serious or light-hearted) and see whether you can find instances where the writer has used certain linguistic <u>techniques</u> (e.g. <u>simile</u> or <u>metaphor</u>) to strengthen their arguments.

When taking revision notes on analysing newspaper reports, as illustrated on page 42, you could write key words in the margin of this handout and then use these key words to help create a **summary list**, like the example below:

ANALYSING NEWSPAPER REPORTS

Different approaches:
a) Think about overall effect on reader
b) Check for bias (opinion / theory v. facts)

Use different colours for each section

2. Focus on certain parts:
a) Headings and sub-headings
b) Content (body of text)
c) Photos and Illustrations + captions

There is no need to write full sentences

3. Examine language used:
a) Tone (light, serious)
b) Linguistic techniques (simile, metaphor)

Include plenty of symbols

Summary Shapes

Another option is to take notes inside or around the sections or parts of a **summary shape**. For example, imagine that the section of your Geography textbook on 'river processes' looks like the passage of text below:

River Processes

ABRASION
ATTRITION
H. ACTION
CORROSION

Erosion – Processes of river erosion include: <u>abrasion</u> (e.g. sediments rubbing against the river bed and sides); <u>attrition</u> (e.g. rocks colliding and breaking into smaller pieces); <u>hydraulic action</u> (e.g. immense force of the water itself causes erosion); and <u>corrosion</u> (e.g. water reacts with or dissolves chemicals in certain rocks, which are then carried downstream in solution).

TRACTION
SALTATION
SUSPENSION
SOLUTION

Transportation – Sediments can be transported along the river bed by <u>traction</u> (e.g. rocks are rolled and pushed along the river bed) and <u>saltation</u> (e.g. large sand grains are bounced along the river bed). In addition, smaller sediments can be carried in <u>suspension</u> (i.e. in water above the river bed) and some minerals are dissolved and carried as <u>solution.</u>

↓ VELOCITY
BENDS
LAKES
SEAS

Deposition – Rivers deposit materials when their <u>velocity is decreased</u> to such an extent that they can no longer carry their entire load. This often occurs on the inside of <u>bends</u> or meanders and when they enter a <u>lake</u> or the <u>sea.</u>

33

When taking revision notes on 'river processes', as illustrated on page 44, you could extract key words and write these in the margins. As there are twelve key processes to remember from this topic, you could then draw a big circle and divide this into twelve parts. Finally, as illustrated below, in each of these parts you could write key words to remind you of different river processes.

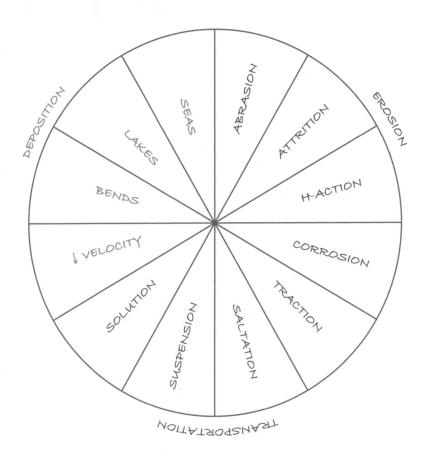

Remember that you can use different shapes. For example, if there had been three river processes then you could have written key words at the end of the three points of a triangle or if there had been four processes you could have drawn symbols inside the sections of a four-part square. If there had been five or six processes then you could have used five-point or six-point stars!

Summary Maps

You can also take revision notes on topics by writing key words and drawing symbols on the branches of a **summary map**. For example, information extracted from notes below (taken during a Food Technology lesson on 'food preservation') could be used to create the summary map on page 47.

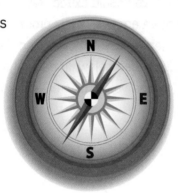

Microorganisms and enzymes that damage food or cause illness are made less active or destroyed by:

-29°C → -18°C
Blast
Fluidised Bed
Immersion

1. FREEZING
Frozen foods must be stored between -29°C (commercial freezers) and -18°C (domestic freezers). Commercial freezing techniques include: blast freezing, fluidised bed freezing and immersion freezing.

VP
MAP
Air Beds/
Chambers
Sugar, Salt

2. REMOVING OXYGEN or WATER
O_2 is removed by Vacuum Packing and replaced by $CO_2 + N_2$ through Modified Atmosphere Packing (MAP). H_2O is removed by drying foods on hot air beds; spraying foods into hot air chambers; or exposing foods to substances (e.g. salt, sugar) that dehydrate them.

Pstrstn:
72°/15s + 10°
Strlstn:
115°/30m
UHT: 130°/1s

3. HEATING
During pasteurisation food is heated to 72°C for 15 seconds and then quickly cooled to 10°C. During sterilisation canned meat/veg are heated to 115°C for 30 minutes. During Ultra Heat Treatment (UHT) food is heated to 130°C for 1 second.

Summary maps can be presented in a 'portrait' layout (as below) or, by turning the page 90° before you start writing, in a 'landscape' layout.

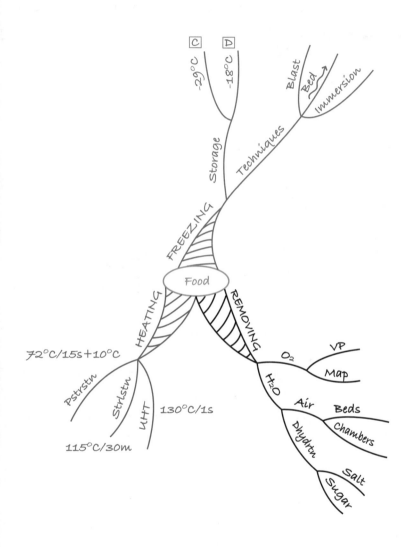

💻 Scan all of your summary shapes and summary maps into your computer so that you can exchange them with friends and so that you have digital copies saved on file.

Mnemonics

Mnemonics are things that help students to remember information. This unit teaches you how to use mnemonics when revising for your exams.

Testing Yourself

- Give yourself 30 seconds to memorise the 15 words listed below and then write down as many as you can remember in any order.
- Read through the story below and then try to tell it to someone else.
- Use your memory of the story to help you try to recall the 15 words a second time.

	At the Airport
Airport Blanket Flags Monk Café Dragon Ice Skull Tea Cards Book Shell Crystal Teeth	Imagine that you wake-up at an **airport** wrapped-up in a **blanket** that is made of **flags**. An old **monk** comes over and quietly whispers that you should go to the **café** upstairs to meet your friends. When you arrive at the café there is a foul-smelling **dragon** sitting on a block of **ice** and opposite him is a beautiful girl sitting on a giant **skull**. They are drinking **tea** and playing **cards**. Suddenly the girl throws a card at you which, when you catch it, transforms into a little **book**. You look up again but the dragon and the girl have vanished. All that is left at their table is a **shell** full of **crystal teeth**!

Using Mnemonics Effectively

You should have found it easier to remember the words on page 48 the second time. This is because having to memorise and recall the story acted as a mnemonic. Five principles to apply when creating mnemonics are summed up by **SOLAR** (**S**ymbols; **O**utstanding; **L**inks; **A**ll five senses; **R**epetition):

Symbols – Information can be stored and communicated by symbols. What thoughts come to mind, for example, when you see a picture of the US flag or a red cross? When creating mnemonics use symbols that are powerful and meaningful to you.

Outstanding – By making things outstanding your mnemonics will be easier to remember. This is why the story on page 48 included an old monk and a dragon.

Links – Including clear links in mnemonics speeds-up recall. For example, the monk took you to a café where you found the girl who threw a card that became a book, etc.

All five senses – The best mnemonics evoke different senses. In the story you should have been able to imagine the **sound** of the monk whispering, the **smell** of the dragon and the **sight** of the crystal teeth.

Repetition – Go back over mnemonics several times. Memorising the story and then telling it to someone else should have made it easier to recall the 15 words.

Example 1: Physics

The waves making up the electromagnetic spectrum can be presented as a continuum, running from those with the shortest wavelength (gamma rays) to those with the longest wavelength (radio waves):

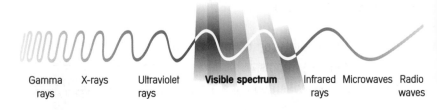

| Gamma rays | X-rays | Ultraviolet rays | **Visible spectrum** | Infrared rays | Microwaves | Radio waves |

To memorise this spectrum, start with an 'anchor symbol' that links to the topic (e.g. all electromagnetic waves **travel** at the same speed through a vacuum so you could use a **jogger** as the anchor symbol). You can then link this anchor symbol to symbols that represent each of the seven electromagnetic waves. For example:

Imagine that you watch a news report about a jogger who was chased by scientists wearing protective clothing (**gamma rays** are emitted by highly dangerous radioactive materials); taken by these scientists to a hospital (**X-rays** are used to check for broken bones); driven from this hospital to a beauty salon for a sun-bed session (**ultraviolet waves** are emitted by sun-beds); seen leaving this salon (we use **visible light** waves to see things) by a burglar alarm salesperson (some burglar alarms use **infrared waves**), who stole his mobile (**microwaves** are used by some mobile phones); and then interviewed about his experience by radio and TV reporters (**radio waves** are used for radio and TV broadcasting).

Example 2: History

The Wall Street Crash is one of the most significant incidents in 20th Century history. Here are a few key events that took place around this time:

1. There was high demand for US goods after the First World War.
2. Certain US industries (e.g. the motor industry) grew rapidly in the early 1920s.
3. The US economy started to decline in the late 1920s.
4. Panic-selling led to the Wall Street Crash in 1929.
5. US banks and companies were forced to close.
6. Widespread poverty resulted, because many people lost their jobs and savings.

To memorise these events you first need to think of an anchor symbol. As the Wall Street Crash took place in America, one option would be to centre your mnemonic around the US flag:

Imagine that a man grabs a US flag (**high demand for American goods**) and sticks it on the top of his huge car (**growth of motor industry**). He then gets into a much smaller car (**decline of the US economy**) and drives-off. He passes through a market where everyone is frantically trying to sell things (**panic-selling**) and hears a huge explosion (**the Wall Street Crash**). The man arrives at a town where every shop is closed (**banks and companies forced to close**) and gives his car to a beggar on the roadside (**widespread poverty**).

Example 3: ICT

During ICT exams, you may need to remember the pros and cons of different methods of communication. Here are five advantages and five disadvantages of using email:

Advantages of Email	Disadvantages of Email
Emails can be sent at any time of day	Private information can easily be forwarded
Computer files can be attached	Content can be misinterpreted
Very swift speed of delivery	Computer might be infected by viruses
Emails can be sent all over the world	You might receive lots of spam
Very low delivery costs	Computer thieves can access old emails

As this topic is about emails you could use a laptop as the anchor symbol:

Imagine that you leave home with your new laptop and the sun's shining (**advantages of email**). You walk to a 24-hour supermarket (**sent any time of day**). You hang your laptop bag on a trolley (**files can be attached**) and dash around the shop (**swift delivery**) picking-up lots of exotic foods (**sent across world**) that cost just 1p in total (**low delivery costs**). When you leave the shop it's pouring with rain (**disadvantages of email**). A complete stranger tells you your bank account details (**private information easily forwarded**) and also that your friend never wants to see you again (**misinterpretation**). You get on the bus to go home and feel unwell (**computer viruses**). Someone tries to sell you a sweet wrapper (**spam**) and a passenger runs off with your laptop (**thieves can access old emails**).

Example 4: Spanish

You can also use mnemonics to help memorise foreign words by splitting these words down into syllables and then using these syllables (or words that sound like them) to create memorable sentences. Here's an example of how this technique could be used to help learn the Spanish words for colours (in Spanish 'j' is pronounced like an English 'h' and 'v' is sometimes pronounced a bit like an English 'b').

RED = ROJO (ROW HO)
The headmaster put his **red** pens in a **row** and shouted '**Ho!** Ho! Ho!'

YELLOW = AMARILLO (ARMADILLO)
All the policemen cried when their boss lost his **yellow armadillo**.

BLUE = AZUL (YOU FOOL)
She stole the **blue** jewel and shouted '**Azul!** You fool!'

GREEN = VERDE (BEAR DAY)
The **green** giant travelled to the milky-way on Grizzly **Bear Day**.

ORANGE = ANARANJADO (ANNA RANG HADO)
Princess **Anna rang Hado** when she saw a strange **orange** shadow.

PINK = ROSA (ROW TSAR)
The bouncer wore **pink** when he agreed to **row** the Russian **Tsar** to see a shrink.

PURPLE = MORADO (MORE HARD DOUGH)
The **purple** priest asked for **more hard dough** at the end of his first show.

BROWN = MARRON (MA RON)
Ma Ron only drank **brown** ale when she worked in that jail.

Revising English

You need to learn how to study different texts (e.g. newspapers, biographies, fiction) for GCSE English. This unit gives examples of how to revise English by looking at the topic 'novels and short stories'.

Studying Novels and Short Stories

Read through the annotated passage of text below about how to study novels and short stories.

CHARACTERS
3 Attributes
Intro + Change!

Characters
Note attributes of the main characters, such as their actions, personality and beliefs. How are they introduced to the reader and how do they change as the plot unfolds?

CONTEXT
Social
Place
Time
Single / Several

Context
Is the novel set in a single social, geographical and historical context (e.g. working class Victorian London) or in several contrasting contexts (e.g. early and late 20th Century India)?

PLOT
123 Sections
🕐 Timescale

Plot
Compare the characters and context in different sections of the plot (e.g. beginning, middle and end). Over what timescale is the story recounted (e.g. one day or a hundred years)?

THEMES
6 Examples
Influence?!

Themes
Identify themes raised by the novel (e.g. attitudes to money, marriage, family, education, morality, feelings of loss). How are your attitudes to these themes influenced by this story?

LANGUAGE
Narrative 1ˢᵗ/3ʳᵈ
Dialogue
Devices

Language
Is the story written from a narrative perspective (e.g. first or third person)? How is dialogue used? Are other devices (e.g. similes and metaphors) used to evoke a particular atmosphere?

Unpicking the Structure

Having annotated this text by underlining key words and writing in the margins (page 54), you could begin revising this topic by quickly sketching-out a summary shape (e.g. a five-point star) that reminds you of the five core sections:

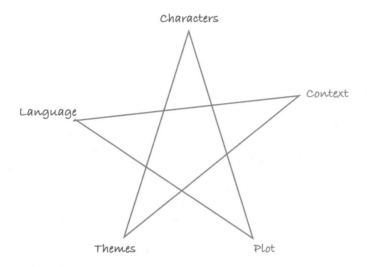

You could then jot down a short summary list that helps you to focus on key points within each of these five sections:

Characters	Attributes (actions, personality, beliefs) How characters are introduced and change
Context	E.g. social, place and time Single context v several contrasting contexts
Plot	Sections (beginning, middle, end) Short v long timescale
Themes	E.g. money, marriage, family, education, morality, loss Influence on reader's attitudes
Language	Narrative perspective (1st person, 3rd person) Dialogue + devices (simile, metaphor) and atmosphere

Summary Map

To create a summary for your revision file, use initial work on the broad structure of this topic to help create a more detailed summary map on how to study novels and short stories:

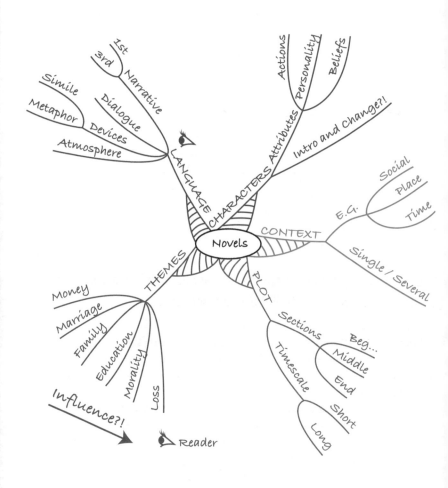

Scan summary maps into your computer as pictures and then use them as 'desktop backgrounds' for your computer screen – this will make it easier to review them.

Reviewing the Topic

To review this topic, a few weeks after creating your notes, you could quickly sketch the branches of your summary map and then try to fill in the branches from memory:

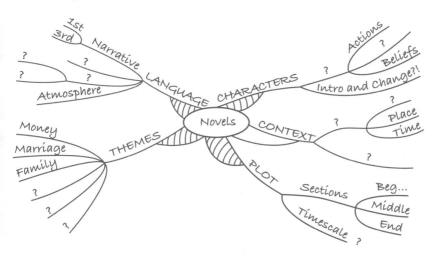

Or you could try to write a short summary of this topic in your own words and then look back at the original to see what you missed out:

Things to look at when studying novels include: characters, context, plot, themes and language. I could examine aspects of the main characters, such as their actions, personalities and beliefs. I might note whether the author sets the story in a single context or several contexts. I could also compare different stages of the plot (e.g. the beginning, middle and end) and note the timescale over which the plot unfolds. In addition, I might look at some of the main themes or check how the author uses dialogue.

How characters are introduced and change

E.g. social context, place and time

Other devices such as simile and metaphor

Revising Maths

To prepare for Maths exams you need to learn how to correctly apply a variety of mathematical procedures and formulae when solving problems. This unit highlights ways of improving your problem-solving skills and shows you how to create Maths summary sheets.

Studying Percentages

Read through the annotated passage of text below about working out percentages.

$\%$

$\underline{cent} = 100^{ths}$

$\dfrac{a \times b}{100}$

$\downarrow \uparrow \%$

Option 1

$b \pm \dfrac{a \times b}{100}$

Option 2

Multiplier

$(1 \pm \dfrac{a}{100})$

Calculating Percentages

Per<u>cent</u> means 'number of <u>hundredths</u>'. So, the question, 'Calculate 8 percent of 400' is actually asking you to 'calculate 8 hundredths of 400'. To answer this question you could, therefore, calculate the value of <u>one hundredth</u> of <u>400</u> and multiply this value by <u>8</u> (i.e. <u>400</u> ÷ <u>100</u> x <u>8</u> = 32).

Expressed in another way, to calculate a percentage '<u>a</u>' of a number '<u>b</u>', you can use the equation $\dfrac{a \times b}{100}$.

Percentage Changes

When an original amount, '<u>b</u>', is increased or decreased by a certain percentage, '<u>a</u>', to calculate the new amount you could:

1. Calculate the change: $\dfrac{a \times b}{100}$

2. Add this to (for an increase) or subtract this from (for a decrease) the original amount '<u>b</u>':

$b \pm (\dfrac{a \times b}{100})$

Another way of calculating the new amount is by multiplying the original amount '<u>b</u>' by 1 ± (plus for increases and minus for decreases) the percentage change '<u>a</u>' divided by 100:

$b \times (1 \pm \dfrac{a}{100})$

(The section of this equation in brackets is known as the multiplier).

The annotated text on page 58 introduces a few key expressions that are used to calculate percentages and percentage changes. Study them carefully for a few minutes. Pay particular attention to the way that the collection of terms ('a', 'b', '100', etc.) making up each formula have been highlighted using different colours. Writing in the margins will help you to remember which formula to apply!

Having worked with Maths texts in this way, to deepen your understanding of topics, jot-down some initial insights on rough paper:

Percentages

The idea of a percentage as 'hundredths' reminds me that Mr Jacobs explained in our Maths lesson that the same number can be <u>expressed</u> as a percentage, fraction or decimal:

Percentages:	Fractions:	Decimals:
150%	150/100 (or 1½!)	1.5
80%	80/100 (or 4/5!)	0.80
25%	25/100 (or ¼!)	0.25

Need to remember that...
   If multiplier <1 then change is a <u>decrease</u>
   If multiplier >1 then change is an <u>increase</u>

...and that the formulae for calculating percentage ↓↑ are really helpful for questions that involve VAT...

   VAT = 17.5%
   → So, if adding VAT, the multiplier will be 1.175.

Creating Summary Sheets

To develop a more detailed single-page overview of your knowledge of this topic you could also create a summary sheet like the example below:

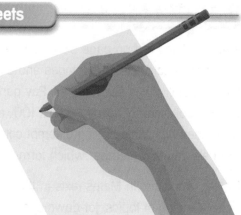

Summary Sheet : Percentages

Calculating the percentage 'a' of the number 'b':

$$\frac{a \times b}{100}$$

Increasing / Decreasing the number 'b' by the percentage 'a':

Option 1:
- Calculate the percentage 'a' of 'b':
$$\frac{a \times b}{100}$$
- Add / Subtract this amount to 'b':
  a) If an increase: $b + (\frac{a \times b}{100})$
  b) If a decrease: $b - (\frac{a \times b}{100})$

E.g. Calculating VAT:
    Selling price = List price + VAT

Option 2:
- Calculate the multiplier:
$$1 \pm \frac{a}{100}$$
- Multiply this by 'b':
$$b \times (1 \pm \frac{a}{100})$$

E.g. Calculating VAT:
VAT multiplier = 1 + (17.5/100) = 1.175
Selling price = List price x 1.175

Testing Your Understanding

The best way to review Maths topics is by trying to answer lots of practice exam questions.

When testing yourself in this way, run through the three problem-solving steps outlined in the example below:

Exam Questions: Percentages

The list price of a laptop (i.e. its price excluding VAT) is £660.
a) Calculate the amount, in pounds, of <u>VAT charged</u> on this item.
b) Calculate its <u>selling price</u>.

Step 1: Underline key words in the questions (see above).

Step 2: Write down some initial notes on rough paper.

17.5% (a) of list price (b) → $\frac{a \times b}{100}$

Option 1: Selling price = list price + VAT

Option 2: Selling price = list price × VAT <u>multiplier</u>

$1 + \frac{a}{100}$

Step 3: Answer the questions showing your workings.

a) VAT charged = $\frac{17.5 \times \text{list price}}{100}$

VAT charged = $\frac{17.5 \times £660}{100}$ = <u>£115.50</u>

b) Selling price = list price × VAT multiplier

VAT multiplier = $1 + \frac{17.5}{100}$ = 1.175

Selling price = £660 × 1.175 = <u>£775.50</u>

Revising Science

To do well in Science exams you need to have a good knowledge and understanding of scientific principles and concepts. You also need to show that you can think and reason scientifically. This unit uses a Chemistry topic to highlight ways of making the most of your Science revision.

Studying Chemistry

Imagine that you took the following notes during a Chemistry lesson. Read through them and look at how they've been annotated.

Solubility
1! HCl, NH$_3$
2! CO$_2$
3! O$_2$

The Solubility of Different Gases

The only two gases that are very soluble in water are hydrogen chloride (HCl) and ammonia (NH$_3$). Carbon dioxide (CO$_2$) is less soluble than hydrogen chloride and ammonia but more soluble than oxygen (O$_2$) – which is only slightly soluble in water.

variables
↓ +Temperature
↑ +Pressure

Variables that Influence Levels of Solubility

The volume of a gas dissolved in water decreases with increasing temperature (°C) and increases with increasing pressure (p).

Acids
CO$_2$ → H$_2$CO$_3$
Alkalis
NH$_3$ → NH$_4$OH

The pH of Solutions

Some gases dissolve in water to form acids. For example, carbon dioxide (CO$_2$) dissolves in water to form the weak acid carbonic acid (H$_2$CO$_3$):

$$CO_2 + H_2O \leftrightharpoons H_2CO_3.$$

Other gases dissolve in water to form alkalis. For example, ammonia dissolves in water to form the alkali ammonium hydroxide (NH$_4$OH):

$$NH_3 + H_2O \rightarrow NH_4OH$$

Identifying Core Concepts

Before taking detailed revision notes, it's helpful to begin studying Science topics by trying to quickly identify and jot down in your own words some of the core concepts that you might need to understand:

Solubility of Gases in Water: Core Concepts

1. First section COMPARES solubility of DIFFERENT gases. Gives EXAMPLES of gases that are very, quite, slightly soluble in water.

2. Second section shows how solubility in water of a SINGLE gas goes up and down according to temperature and pressure.

3. Third section highlights that the SOLUTIONS created vary in their pH. Gives EXAMPLES of acids and alkalis.

Creating a Summary Shape

You can then use key words and symbols from the annotated passage of text on page 62 to help create a summary shape that records key points from this topic:

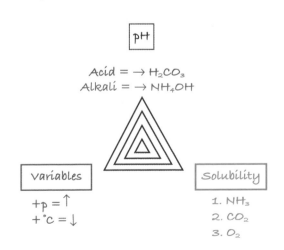

pH

Acid $= \rightarrow H_2CO_3$
Alkali $= \rightarrow NH_4OH$

Variables
$+p = \uparrow$
$+ °c = \downarrow$

Solubility
1. NH_3
2. CO_2
3. O_2

Creating a Detailed Summary

If you have time, you could also create a more detailed summary map of this topic to put in your revision file:

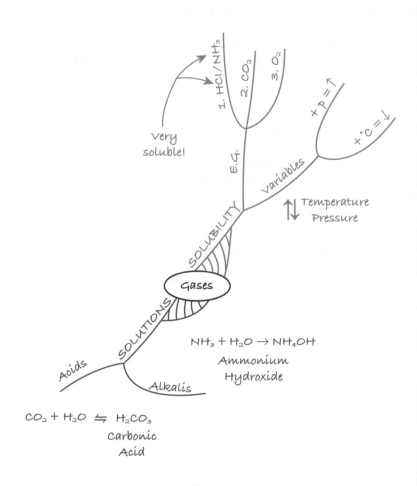

Reviewing the Topic

To review this topic, a few days or weeks after you take your notes, you could try to recall your summary shape – or you could sketch out the branches of your summary map and then try to fill in these from memory. You could also have a go at answering practice exam questions related to this topic. For example:

1. Rank the following three gases from most soluble to least soluble in $100cm^3$ of water under identical conditions of temperature and pressure:

2	Carbon dioxide (CO_2)
3	Oxygen (O_2)
1	Ammonia (NH_3)

2. Temperature and pressure alter the amount of gas dissolved in water. Under which of the following conditions would the most gas dissolve in $100cm^3$ of water?

	High temperature and high pressure
	Low temperature and low pressure
✓	Low temperature and high pressure
	High temperature and low pressure

3. Explain why a solution of ammonia in water turns blue when litmus is added.

   When ammonia dissolves in water it actually reacts with the water to create ammonium hydroxide: $NH_3 + H_2O \rightarrow NH_4OH$. This substance is an alkali so the solution created turns blue when litmus is added.

Revising Modern Languages –

This unit highlights techniques that will help you to learn vocabulary, use different tenses and construct complex sentences when revising Modern Foreign Languages. Although all of the examples in this unit are French, you can use the same principles and skills to learn any language.

Language Themes

GCSE Modern Foreign Languages courses are typically organised into a collection of themes, such as:

- Health
- Holidays
- Self and family
- Leisure
- In the town
- The world at large
- Work and future plans

Each of these themes has a set of vocabulary that you'll need to learn (e.g. words for different sports in 'Leisure' and words for different family members in 'Self and family'). It's also common for GCSE examiners to ask you to complete particular tasks related to each theme (e.g. as part of spoken exams, to talk about what you did during your holidays last year and what you plan to do during your holidays next year).

One way of organising your revision is to set aside time to focus on practising tasks and revising vocabulary related to each theme. Remember that this will require you to practise using different tenses. You'll also need to learn not only how to translate from the target language into English (e.g. for listening and reading exams), but also how to translate from English into the target language (e.g. for spoken and written exams).

Learning Vocabulary

When learning vocabulary related to each of the themes in your syllabus, use tables to divide words into sub-sets. In the example below, French words related to the theme 'Self and family' have been arranged into six sub-sets and colours have been used to differentiate words according to gender (i.e. blue for masculine words and red for feminine words). Create similar tables in both French (or whatever language you're revising) and English so that you can test your vocabulary.

PARENTS	SIBLINGS	GRANDPARENTS
Les parents	Le jumeau	Les grands-parents
La mère	La jumelle	La grand-mère
La maman	La sœur	La petite-fille
Le père	La demi-sœur	Le grand-père
Le papa	Le frère	Le petit-fils
	Le demi-frère	
EXTENDED FAMILY	IN-LAWS	MARITAL STATUS
Le cousin	Les beaux-parents	Le fiancé
La cousine	La belle-mère	La fiancée
La tante	La belle-sœur	La femme
La nièce	Le beau-père	L'epouse
L'oncle	Le beau-frère	Le mari
Le neveu		L'epoux

All the words in the table above are nouns. You can, of course, also create other tables for verbs, adjectives and adverbs.

Using Different Tenses

Students that get the best marks in GCSE Modern Foreign Language exams show that they can use a range of tenses when listening, speaking, reading and writing. Practise using different tenses by creating a table with 'past', 'present' and 'future' columns like the one below – in this case, all of the phrases relate to the GCSE French topic 'Holidays and accommodation':

Past	Present	Future
I worked at a café. J'ai travaillé dans un café.	I work at a café. Je travaille dans un café.	I will work at a café. Je travaillerai dans un café.
She went skiing in Italy. Elle est allée faire du ski en Italie.	She is skiing in Italy. Elle fait du ski en Italie.	She will go skiing in Italy. Elle ira faire du ski en Italie.
The hotel was great. L'hôtel était génial.	The hotel is great. L'hôtel est génial.	The hotel will be great. L'hôtel sera génial.
We bought souvenirs. Nous avons acheté des souvenirs.	We are buying souvenirs. Nous achetons des souvenirs.	We will buy souvenirs. Nous achèterons des souvenirs.
They visited Madrid. Ils ont visité Madrid.	They are visiting Madrid. Ils visitent Madrid.	They will visit Madrid. Ils visiteront Madrid.

>> If you feel confident, create additional columns to practise using other tenses, such as the imperfect tense.

Using More Complex Sentences

Examiners also give higher marks to students who answer using complex (rather than simple) sentences. A fun way to practise constructing complex sentences is by playing 'language lottery':

- Write out all the nouns and verbs that you need to know related to a particular theme (e.g. 'leisure') on individual scraps of paper.
- Put all the nouns in one bag and all the verbs in another.
- Now, pick out a few nouns and a few verbs (say three nouns and two verbs).
- Use all of these words to construct a sentence.

For example, if you picked out the following five words...

...then you might create this sentence:

> J'aime écouter de la musique après l'école, et pendant le weekend je vais au cinéma ou je joue au tennis avec mon père.
> I enjoy listening to music after school, and at weekends I go to the cinema or I play tennis with my Dad.

You can use similar techniques to write passages of text that examiners ask for in exams, such as a postcard to an imaginary pen-friend or a letter applying for a job. Remember to use several tenses.

Revising Geography

When revising Geography you need to develop a good knowledge and understanding of a wide range of physical, human and environmental forces, systems and processes. This unit helps you to study and revise Geography.

Obstacles to Development

The text below relates to the topic 'development' and outlines some of the obstacles faced by development projects that aim to improve the living standards of people in Less Economically Developed Countries (LEDCs). Have a look at how this has been structured and annotated.

↓Employment
↓Income levels
=↓Taxes
☹ Infrastructure
☹ P-Services

Economic – Employment and income levels are low so governments don't collect the taxes required to invest in infrastructure (e.g. roads, power stations) or public services (e.g. hospitals, schools).

£?! Systems
Water!!
☹ Health Ed
↓♀ Expectancies

Health – Under-funded health systems (e.g. a lack of clinics, doctors and equipment), unclean water supplies and poor health education contribute to the low life expectancies in LEDCs.

↓Y Schooling
Illiteracy
↓Skills
☹ PAL

Educational – Many people don't go to school, or leave school at a young age, which leads to high levels of illiteracy, few people developing the skills needed to work in higher paid jobs and, in general, an inadequate preparation for adult life.

Droughts!
Floods!
Hurricanes!
Earthquakes!

Environmental – Many LEDCs are situated in areas of the world that are highly prone to environmental crises such as droughts, floods, hurricanes and earthquakes.

Identifying the Essentials

Having annotated the passage of text on page 70 you could begin to improve your knowledge and understanding of this topic by identifying single words or phrases that link to an essential issue or concept discussed in each paragraph.

Paragraph	Essential Concept / Issue
1.	Tax Collection
2.	Life Expectancy
3.	Preparation for Adult Life
4.	Environmental Crisis

For example:

1. The first paragraph identifies two causes (i.e. low levels of employment and low incomes) and two consequences (i.e. lack of investment in infrastructure and lack of investment in public services) of the inadequate **taxes** collected by governments in LEDCs.

2. The second paragraph lists a number of factors (e.g. under-funding of health systems, a lack of clean water and poor health education) that contribute to the low **life expectancies** of people living in LEDCs.

3. The third paragraph outlines two issues (i.e. some children not going to school at all and many other children leaving school at a young age) that contribute to two examples (i.e. illiteracy and lack of vocational expertise) of how LEDCs fail to offer young people sufficient **preparation for adult life**.

4. The fourth paragraph highlights four **environmental crises** (i.e. droughts, floods, hurricanes and earthquakes) that are more common in parts of the world where LEDCs are situated.

Focusing on the Details

Having developed a broad understanding of the structure of this topic, you can now use this to help create a summary for your revision file that records more of the details from the passage of text on page 70:

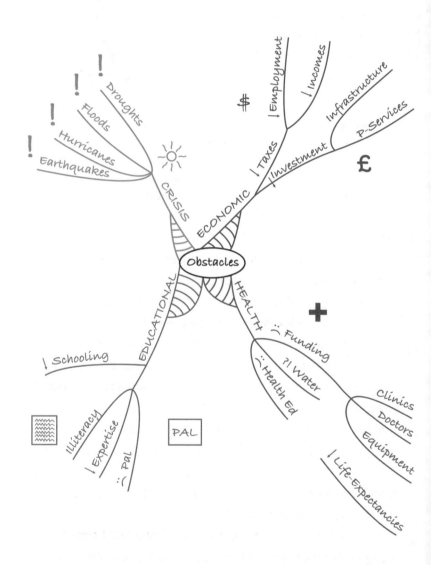

Questions and Answers

To review this topic you could organise a short 'questions and answers' session with a family member or a friend. During this review session they could ask you questions about information in the original passage of text and then they could add to, or correct, your responses. Your discussion might, for example, run something like this:

'OK then, what are some of the consequences of the fact that LEDCs' governments find it difficult to collect taxes?'

'Well, this means that the governments don't have much money to invest in infrastructure such as roads or power stations, or in public services such as schools and hospitals'.

'Excellent! Tell me some specific things then about the consequences of under-funding of health systems in LEDCs.'

'They don't train enough doctors'.

'Yeah. That's correct but you could also mention that there aren't enough clinics or medical equipment'. What else influences the life expectancies of people living in LEDCs?'

'The lack of clean water'.

'Also poor health education. And what about the education system in LEDCs? What sorts of educational issues do LEDCs face?'

'The fact that some children don't go to school at all and loads of others only stay in school for a few years means that illiteracy rates are high, not many people develop the expertise needed to get higher paid 'professional' jobs and so, generally, young people aren't prepared fully for adult life'.

Revising History

When revising History you'll need to develop a good memory and understanding of forces shaping events in Britain and abroad over the last hundred years or more. This unit helps you to make the most of your History revision.

Birth of the Welfare State

The text below identifies public services that the British government dramatically improved after the end of World War II. As you read through this, think about how you might create revision notes on this topic.

Accident/Injury
Sickness
Unemployment
Old Age
Bereavement

Social Security – All workers were expected to pay money into a national insurance (<u>NI</u>) scheme that provided benefits and pensions to people suffering as a result of: <u>accident or injury</u>; <u>sickness</u>; <u>unemployment</u>; <u>old age</u> or <u>bereavement</u>.

GPs, Hospitals
Drugs
Opticians
Dentists
Maternity
Child Welfare

Healthcare – The establishment of the National Health Service (<u>NHS</u>) led to a system that gave citizens free <u>GP appointments</u>, <u>hospital treatments</u>, <u>eye-care</u>, <u>dentistry</u>, <u>prescription drugs</u>, <u>maternity services</u> and <u>child welfare services</u>.

700,000 + H
Replacements
↑M + ↑B
14 New Towns

Housing – Over <u>700,000</u> new houses were built to <u>replace those destroyed</u> during the war and to meet rising <u>demand</u>, due to an increase in <u>marriages</u> and <u>birth rates</u> after the war. The government developed <u>14 'New Towns'</u> in the UK.

EA 1944
Free 2° Ed
14→15 Years

Education – Following the Education Act of <u>1944</u>, <u>free</u> secondary education was made available to all and the <u>school leaving age</u> was raised from <u>14 to 15</u>.

Option 1: Linear Notes

When constructing a single-page summary of this topic for your revision file, you could create a summary list something like the example below:

SOCIAL SECURITY

National Insurance (NI) provided benefits / pensions:
- Unemployment
- Accident / Injury or Sickness
- Old Age
- Bereavement

HEALTHCARE

The National Health Service (NHS) provided free:
- GPs, hospitals, drugs
- Opticians + Dentists
- Maternity services
- Child welfare services

HOUSING

700,000 + new houses built:
- 14 New towns
- Replaced those destroyed in war
- Due to rising demand ← ↑ marriages / births

EDUCATION

- Education Act 1944
- Free 2° Education 4 all
- School leaving age: increased from 14 → 15 Years

 Make summary lists in Microsoft Word™ so that you can easily change colours and import clip-art etc.

Option 2: Summary Maps

Another option would be to create a summary map:

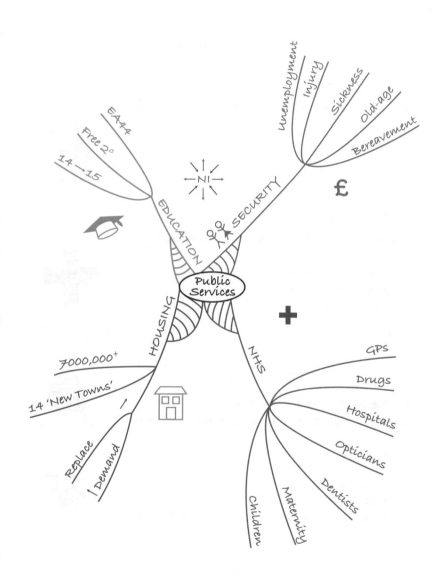

Reviewing this Topic

To review this aspect of your History syllabus, you could write down a few key words or phrases from your revision notes and then use these to try to write about sections of this topic in your own words.

For example, let's say that you chose...

1 Old age
2 National Health Service
3 Rising Demand
4 Education Act 1944

...then you could write:

Old Age
Soon after WWII the government used NI contributions to pay pensions to the elderly. People could also apply for benefits if they were unemployed, injured, sick or bereaved.

National Health Service
The creation of the NHS meant that for the first time everyone could benefit from FREE health services such as: appointments with doctors; hospitals; eye-care; dentistry; maternity and child welfare services.

Rising Demand
Rising demand for housing resulted from more marriages and higher birth rates. Alongside the need to replace houses destroyed during the war, this led to the construction of over 700,000 new houses and to the creation of 14 new towns.

Education Act 1944
The Education Act 1944 led to free secondary education for all and to the school leaving age changing from 14 to 15.

Coursework Projects

Many GCSE courses now encourage or require students to complete research projects as part of their coursework. This unit offers advice that will help you to plan, conduct and write-up your research.

Clarifying Your Aims

Before reflecting on how you might set about collecting and analysing data, begin to plan your research project by clarifying its focus and aims. For example, when planning your Geography coursework you might:

1. **Link your research project to a topic** – All of the topics in your Geography syllabus are categorised as: physical geography, human geography or environmental geography. You'd like to work in the tourism industry when you leave college, so you decide to focus on an issue related to the topic 'tourism' in the 'human geography' section of your syllabus.

2. **Focus on an issue (or set of issues) related to this topic** – Your town used to be a very popular tourist destination but the number of visitors has dropped dramatically over the last twenty years. You decide to use your research to focus on the issue of how your town can attract more tourists again.

3. **Outline the aims of your research as a question (or questions)** – 'What do people working in the tourism industry in a British seaside resort think can be done to attract more visitors to this declining, but once popular, tourist destination?'

4. **Construct a provisional title for your coursework report** – 'Reversing the fortunes of the tourism industry in a British seaside resort'.

Sampling the Population

When attempting to develop a better understanding about the population that you're researching (e.g. everyone working in the tourist industry in your town), due to time and financial constraints, you won't be able to collect data from the whole population. Instead, you'll need to choose a **sample**. For example:

- If you wanted to gain insights into experiences of bullying amongst all the students at your school you might ask a sample of 50 students to complete questionnaires and you might interview a sample of four students in your Year.
- If you wanted to examine the number of people shopping at different times of day in an out-of-town shopping centre, you might record the number of people entering two particular shops between 9am and 5pm on two consecutive days.

Some Ethical Considerations

There are also a range of ethical issues to consider when carrying out research:

Consent: Always receive consent from individuals before involving them in your research (e.g. ask for permission before you record interviews).

Confidentiality: Ensure that contributions are confidential (e.g. highlight that there's no need for participants to write their names on questionnaires, and use pseudonyms if you transcribe interviews).

Consequences: Minimise the negative consequences of your research (e.g. disruption to participants' lives).

Data Collection: Questionnaires

Here are some hints and tips on how to design questionnaires:

Introduction

At the top of the questionnaire, highlight the purpose of your research and point out that responses will remain anonymous. This paragraph can be followed by a few non-threatening questions (e.g. gender, age and ethnicity of respondents).

Question Types

Closed questions have a limited number of responses (e.g. 'Circle the number next to the statement below that most closely matches your views on recycling').

Open questions invite longer and more personal responses (e.g. 'What do you think of the training that people receive when they first join this company?').

Questions to Avoid

Certain types of questions should be avoided:

Leading questions, e.g. 'Would you agree that most men are terrible cooks?'

Complex questions, e.g. 'Are British citizens experiencing post-colonial angst?'

Double negatives, e.g. 'Would you prefer this school to stop people from not wearing school uniform?

Several questions in the same question, e.g. 'Do you enjoy reading newspapers and watching television?'

Data Collection: Interviews

The data that you collect using questionnaires will help you to gain broad insights into characteristics of the populations that you're studying. To supplement or build upon these insights you can use interviews (typically only involve a single individual) and focus groups (typically conducted with groups of 3–6 individuals).

Interview Schedules

Arrive at interviews with an interview schedule that lists-out:
1. Core questions to ask ALL interviewees.
2. Probing questions that you only ask when you want to probe further into particular interviewees' thoughts on certain issues.

Here are a few core questions and probing questions that you might ask during interviews about students' opinions of the lunches at your school:

1. **Core Question:** What do you think of lunches at this school?
   Probing Question: How would you feel if they offered healthy options?
   Probing Question: What was the food like when you first started at this school?
2. **Core Question:** How could the school lunches be improved?
   Probing Question: Give some examples of foods that you'd prefer.
   Probing Question: How do you feel about the idea of banning junk food on certain days?

Make Recordings

If possible, record interviews so that you can transcribe interesting statements made by interviewees. Later on you'll be able to use these to back-up the conclusions in your research report.

Data Analysis

There are two types of data:
quantitative and **qualitative**.

Quantitative data: Responses to closed questions in questionnaires.

1. You ask 20 pupils to answer 'yes' or 'no' to the question, 'Have you ever been bullied by someone at this school?'. Eight pupils answer 'yes' and twelve answer 'no'. You report these findings as percentages:

   $8 / 20 \times 100 = 40\%$ claimed they had been bullied.
   $12 / 20 \times 100 = 60\%$ claimed they hadn't been bullied.

2. You ask 50 pupils, 'Write a number between 1 and 5 that represents how happy you are at this school (5 = very happy; 1 = very unhappy)'. Ten pupils write '5', thirty write '4' and ten write '2'. You report that the mean response (3.8) suggests that most pupils are happy at this school:

   TOTAL: $50 (5 \times 10) + 120 (4 \times 30) + 20 (2 \times 10) = 190$
   Mean response: $190 / 50$ respondents $= 3.8$

Qualitative data: Responses to interview questions and to open questions in questionnaires can be analysed by grouping statements into themes. For example, when you ask pupils, 'What do you think of Citizenship lessons?', their responses suggest that they view Citizenship as a 'free period':

P1: 'You can do what you want in Citizenship. It's like a free period.'
P2: 'During Citizenship you can chill-out and relax.'
P3: 'Most people don't take Citizenship seriously - they see it as free time when they can just doss about.'

Writing-Up Reports

Research reports are typically
divided into five core sections:

1 Introduction – Begin your report with an outline of your research
aims and with a discussion of concepts / issues relating to your
chosen area of focus that you've studied at school (e.g. during
lessons) or through your own reading.

2 Methods – Clarify the methods that you used to collect data (e.g.
questionnaires, interviews) and explain how you analysed data
(e.g. grouping statements into themes).

3 Results – Use a variety of visual representations (e.g. tables,
pie-charts, histograms and scatter diagrams) to help summarise
and highlight key facts, figures and themes that emerged during
data analysis.

4 Conclusions – Link findings to your research aims so that you can
draw tentative conclusions. Highlight the constraints that you faced
(e.g. limited time / money and ethical considerations). Critically,
reflect on how you planned, conducted and wrote-up your
research and identify improvements that you could make if you
conducted a similar research project in the future.

5 Appendices – Include copies of your research instruments (e.g.
questionnaires and interview schedules) in the appendices.

You could use templates from Microsoft Publisher™ to help
design the cover and overall layout of your coursework report.

Exam Technique

There are specific things that you can practise to maximise your performance in the exam room. This unit teaches you how to combat stress and anxiety, and how to perfect the routines and techniques that you apply during exams.

The Effects of Exam Stress

Research shows that the intensity of our mental and emotional response to complex tasks (e.g. taking GCSE exams) can have a **big** effect on task performance. The lowest levels of performance are associated to very low (e.g. lethargy) and very high (e.g. stress and anxiety) intensities of response. Conversely, high performers tend to be better at keeping themselves relaxed and focused.

| Lethargic and depressed | Relaxed and focused | Anxious and stressed |

Intensity of mental and emotional response

The Causes of Exam Stress

You can combat the physical causes of exam stress (e.g. tiredness) by sticking to a positive health and fitness regime, and you can combat the psychological causes of exam stress (e.g. fears of the unknown) by completely familiarising yourself with the whole exam process. The next couple of pages look at each of these 'stress-busters' in more detail.

Health and Fitness Essentials

You can't afford to take risks with your health during the exam period. Alongside the general advice on health and fitness in the Stress Management unit (see page 21), here are some tips on looking after yourself between exams:

Exercise regularly

Set aside 30–60 minutes a day for physical exercise. Avoid activities that are strenuous and, instead, engage in light forms of exercise that keep you supple and fresh. Here are a few examples:

- Stretch for 5–10 minutes every morning.
- Swim at the local pool twice a week.
- Go for a walk with a friend every Sunday.
- Jog around a local park after you get home from school.
- Attend yoga classes one evening a week.

Drink plenty of water

Your memory and concentration levels significantly improve if you drink plenty of water. To keep yourself hydrated, rather than drinking large volumes of water in one go, it's best to take regular sips from a bottle that you carry in your bag and keep on your desk. Find out in advance whether your school allows students to take bottles of water into the exam room.

Go to bed early

Your performance during the exams will suffer if you're tired, so make sure that you get to bed early the night before exams.

Fears of the Unknown

Develop a relaxed and focused approach to your exams by familiarising yourself with key aspects of the exam process.

The exam room

Go to the room (or rooms) where you'll take your exams several weeks before your first exam. Think about your experience of your mocks and what helps you to stay relaxed and focused in this environment. Would you find it useful to arrive at school really early on exam days? Do you prefer to chat to friends or to quietly settle your mind just before invigilators open the exam doors?

Exam papers

Have a look through lots of practice exam papers and past exam papers for each subject that you're taking. Pay attention especially to:

- Initial instructions and guidance
- The number of different sections
- Sections that are optional and sections that are compulsory
- Question types (e.g. multiple choice, short answer, long answer)
- Topics or questions that crop-up most years
- The marking scheme.

Exam conditions

Practise completing sections of past / practice exam papers (or even whole papers) under exam conditions (e.g. without talking to anyone, without a break and within the amount of time specified). Get used to planning or rehearsing answers and to writing at pace.

Answer the Question

Misreading an exam question can lose you lots of marks. Perhaps the most important piece of advice to remember and apply when taking your exams is, therefore, to answer the questions that you've actually been asked.

Command Words

To ensure you answer the question asked, practise identifying command words (e.g. 'describe', 'explain', 'compare', 'choose', 'list', 'why', 'how') in questions from exam papers. For example:

1 **What** effect is this advert trying to have on people that read it?

2 **How** has the author used language to offer insights into the personality of the character introduced in this text?

3 **Describe** and **explain** what happens when bromine water is added to a solution of ascorbic acid.

4 **Explain** why farmers put ammonium sulphate on fields and why this should not be done when heavy rain is forecast.

5 **What** does Source A tell us about how people felt about being asked to fight at the beginning of the First World War?

6 **How** useful is the source in explaining why so many people initially believed that the First World War would be won within a few months?

7 **Describe** the work done by the Sales and Marketing Department in this business.

8 **Suggest** and **explain** three factors that the Directors might consider when deciding how to price this product.

Longer-Answer Questions

Before responding to longer-answer questions, jot down an outline of the structure and content of your answer. For example, if a question in your History exam asks you to, 'Describe improvements that were made to British public services between 1945 and 1951', then you could plan your answer by quickly sketching out from memory a rough outline of the summary map on page 76:

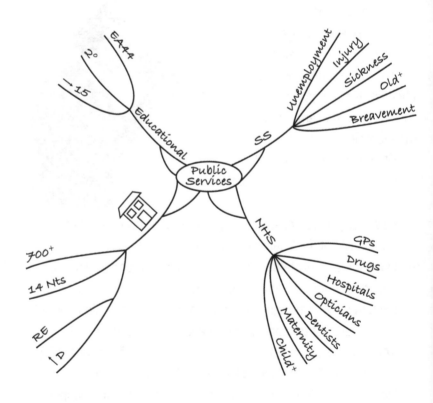

Here are some other ways to get top marks for responses to longer-answer questions:

- Include at least one key point in each paragraph.
- Define any complex words that you use.
- Back up your arguments with examples.
- Write thorough answers, but don't waffle.

Making Final Checks

Always set aside 5–10 minutes towards the end of each exam to complete final checks. During this time:

- Check that you've answered every question. Even if you don't have time to write full answers, examiners may give you additional marks for last-minute responses. It's especially important to respond to all multiple choice questions, because you normally have a 15%–25% chance of guessing the right answer!
- Ensure that your responses actually answer the questions that you've been asked, and that they're as precise and thorough as possible.
- Remember that you can be marked up and down according to your spellings, punctuation, grammar and the overall fluency or impact of your writing style.
- Make sure that you've clearly outlined all of your workings when answering Maths and Science questions.
- If you finish early then don't just sit back and have a quick nap! Check through the whole exam paper to identify further improvements that you can make to your answers.

After Each Exam...

Immediately after you complete an exam paper chat through with friends how you felt you got on – but then close this chapter in the exam process and begin to focus on your next exam.

Revision Strategy

Having read through this whole book, use the advice that you've been offered to create a short and simple revision strategy that outlines how you intend to prepare for your exams. One option would be to create a six-paged document that focuses on: 1) goals; 2) time; 3) health; 4) revision notes; 5) exam technique; and 6) getting started.

Goals

On the first page of your revision strategy write down all of the subjects that you're taking and the very best grades that you believe you can get in each of these subjects.

Subject	Grade
Art	
Business Studies	
Design and Technology	
English	
French	
Geography	
History	
ICT	
Maths	
Science	

Once you've created and completed a table like the one above, check to make sure that you've been optimistic. These are your revision goals – so aim high!

Time

Having completed the exercises in the Time Management unit of this book (see pages 12–17), use the second page of your revision strategy to focus on how best to manage your time. This page should include:

1 An outline of the changes you've decided to make to your daily routine.

WEEKDAY ROUTINE
- Get-up half an hour earlier so that, before I go to school, I can review topics that I revised the night before.
- Spend less time watching TV, so that I complete at least 1 hour of revision per night (e.g. 8–9 p.m.)

WEEKEND ROUTINE
- Quit my Saturday job for a few months, so that I can complete a couple of hours of revision on Saturday mornings.
- Revise with friends once a fortnight (e.g. for an hour or two before going into town on Saturdays).

---

2 A brief summary of how you plan to create revision timetables:

REVISION TIMETABLES
- Every Sunday evening, make a new timetable for the week ahead.
- Remember that, on average, I have committed to revise for 1 hour per day on weekday evenings and 2 hours per day at weekends.
- Distribute time fairly across all subjects / topics.

Health and Fitness

On the third page of your revision strategy, make commitments relating to how you intend to keep yourself fit and healthy during the run-up to your exams.

TAKE MORE EXERCISE

Activities to include in my new '30 minutes a day' exercise regime:

- Stretch for 5–10 minutes first-thing in the morning.
- Take the dog for a walk after I get home from school.
- Go jogging with Charlie on Tuesday and Thursday evenings.
- Swim, play tennis or go for walks at weekends.

CHANGE MY DIET

Some changes that I plan to make to my diet:

Consume LESS	Consume MORE
Fizzy Drinks	Water
Chips	Green Vegetables
Coffee	Herbal Tea
Sugary Snacks	Cooked Meals

REST AND RELAXATION

Ways that I can rest and relax:

- Be in bed by 10.30 on weekdays.
- Socialise with friends on Saturdays and Sundays.
- Always take a 5–10 minute break after an hour of revision.
- Set aside at least an hour every day as my personal 'sanctuary'.

Revision Notes

Use the fourth page of your revision strategy to outline how you intend to structure and organise your file of revision notes.

MY REVISION FILE

PART 1: Revision strategy

To remind myself of how I plan to prepare for my exams, I'll keep a copy of these six pages at the front of my revision file. Once a week I'll have a look through them to reflect on how I'm getting on.

PART 2: Summary sheets

I'll use a range of note-taking techniques (e.g. summary lists, shapes and maps) to build up a single-page summary of each of the topics in each subject that I'm taking. There are 235 topics across all my subjects so this part of my file will eventually hold 235 pieces of paper.

PART 3: Exam papers

I'll keep a copy of past exam papers in the final section of my revision file, so that I can familiarise myself with their structure / content. I need to check with my teachers, though, whether the format of any of these is changing this year compared to previous years.

Items to purchase: 1) a big file; 2) file dividers; 3) a pack of fine-point coloured pens (from the Art shop); 4) plain A4 and A3 paper.

The Exams

To develop a clear awareness of the exam schedule (and to ensure that you remember when to turn up!), include the dates and times of all of your exams on page 5 of your revision file (the ones below are just a short imaginary example – so you'll need to create your own table). You can also use this page to write a check-list of things to remember when taking your exams.

Dates and Times

Subject	Length	Date	Date
ICT	2 hours	20th May	9am
Food Technology	1½ hours	22nd May	1pm
Maths	1½ hours	2nd June	9am
History	2 hours	3rd June	1pm
English	2 hours	5th June	9am
Business Studies	2 hours	10th June	9am
Geography	2 hours	12th June	1pm
Science	2 hours	20th June	9am

Exam Checklist

1. Read the instructions carefully.
2. Take care to answer the questions that have actually been asked.
3. Clearly outline your workings in Maths and Science exams.
4. Answer every question (unless you're instructed otherwise).
5. Set aside time at the end of the exam to check your answers.

Five-Day Plan

Conclude with a five-day revision plan that you can use to make a fresh start or just to get some additional revision under your belt.

DAY ONE
Get up 30 minutes earlier than normal to take the dog for a walk before school. When I get home, take a short break and then revise a topic from my favourite subject for an hour. Go to bed early.

DAY TWO
Get up early to review my notes for the topic that I revised yesterday. Meet up with Sam to revise together for an hour after school. Complete a positive visualisation exercise before bed.

DAY THREE
Continue with my 'early-bird' routine. After school, revise a Science topic and then complete some practice exam questions related to this.

DAY FOUR
Same morning routine. Go to school with a short list of questions to ask teachers relating to sections of particular topics that I don't understand. Meet up with Sam again to revise together after school.

DAY FIVE
In the morning, review all the notes that I took this week and, after school, write an entry in my revision diary about how the week has gone. Take-off the rest of the day to meet-up with friends.

Wishing you every success in your GCSE exams!

Acknowledgements ———

Cover	©Shutterstock.com / Vaju Ariel
p.4	©iStockphoto.com
p.7	©iStockphoto.com / Helle Bro Clemmensen
p.8	©iStockphoto.com / Helle Bro Clemmensen
p.9	©iStockphoto.com / Russell Tate
p.9	©iStockphoto.com / Joshua Blake
p.11	©iStockphoto.com / Stephen Dumayne
p.14	©iStockphoto.com / Paul iJsendoorn
p.16	©iStockphoto.com / Helle Bro Clemmensen
p.18	©iStockphoto.com / Joshua Blake
p.21	©iStockphoto.com / Paolo Tomasso
p.22	©iStockphoto.com / Joshua Blake
p.22	©iStockphoto.com / Lisa McDonald
p.29	©iStockphoto.com / Paul iJsendoorn
p.29	©istockphoto.com / Justin Welzien
p.31	©iStockphoto.com / Christos Georghiou
p.31	©iStockphoto.com / Helle Bro Clemmensen
p.31	©iStockphoto.com / Kim Bryant
p.36	©iStockphoto.com / Kim Bryant
p.36	©iStockphoto.com / Mark Stay
p.38	©iStockphoto.com / Kim Bryant
p.44	Drawn by Andy Roberts at 2idesign
p.46	©iStockphoto.com / Erik van den Berg
p.54	©iStockphoto.com / Kim Bryant
p.67	©iStockphoto.com / Christos Georghiou
p.67	©iStockphoto.com / Helle Bro Clemmensen
p.73	©iStockphoto.com / Joshua Blake
p.77	©istockphoto.com / Justin Welzien
p.79	©iStockphoto.com / Joshua Blake
p.80	©istockphoto.com / Ayaaz Rattansi
p.83	©iStockphoto.com / Miroslaw Pieprzyk
p.89	©iStockphoto.com / Kim Freitas
p.91	©iStockphoto.com / Russell Tate

All other images ©2009 Jupiterimages Corporation and Letts Educational.